INNER SKY

Copyright © 2015 Lori Desrosiers
Paperback ISBN: 978-1-941783-04-7

All rights reserved: except for the purpose of quoting brief passages for review, no part of this book may be reproduced or transmitted in any form or by any means, electronic or mechanical, including photocopying, recording, or by any information storage and retrieval system, without permission in writing from the publisher.

Cover Image : "Flying Toward a Secret Sky," Pd Lietz
Author Photo: Michelle Sutton
Cover design: Steven Asmussen
Design & Layout: Steven Asmussen
Copyediting: Elizabeth Nichols

Glass Lyre Press, LLC.
P.O. Box 2693
Glenview, IL 60026

www.GlassLyrePress.com

INNER SKY

POEMS BY
LORI DESROSIERS

To my daughters Margot and Gabrielle, who are the bravest women I know, and to my mother Blanche, with gratitude.

Contents

Airless   11
   Inertia   13
   Airless   14
   The House in Baldwin   15
   Bitter Beets   16
   An egg breaks   17
   Her Mind Goes Back   18
   The Audio Engineer   19

Out of the Frying Pan   21
   Divorce Rondelet   23
   The Long "Y"   24
   The Grandmother's Story   25
   The Pin   26
   Obituary for a Marriage   28
   the cat   29

Awakening   31
   I need you to   33
   The Corner of the Pantry   34
   Inner Sky   35
   The Ice Crow   36
   New Season   37

Acknowledgments   39

About the Author   41

AIRLESS

Inertia

A strange comfort overtakes you.
Your mind a quiet place,
you just sit —
a hushed audience
waiting for fireworks.

Airless

> A few diehard physicists pointed out that wings are of no propulsive help in airless void.
> — Robert Silverberg, *Earth is the Strangest Planet*

You rendered me airless
in the 1980's when the airwaves
carried new wave music
Elvis Costello and the Clash
an outrush of breath
all that pumped-up love
ten years and two babies worth
blown away in one storm
the resulting flight
yours instead of ours.
Winged your way to the city
where crowds compete for air
and weak trees suspire, barely.
I aired out the house
unpacked my long-tucked wings
and slowly relearned to breathe.

The House in Baldwin

This is where I held
you as a baby
that small white house
with blue trim.
I brought you home
from the hospital
to unfinished upstairs
insulation hanging down
fiberglass stinging air.
He was supposed to finish it
before he left.

Bitter Beets

Some days life is bitter beets
like the white ones
I thought were red
so cooked them up anyway.
The bitterness
colored everything.
Didn't I know
what I was hungry for?

An egg breaks

An egg breaks if you drop it.
A woman breaks
if you twist her words
if you push her too far
she will have to
piece herself back together
without even a recipe.
Don't ever break a woman.
Stick to eggs.

Her Mind Goes Back

Her mind goes back
but she bats it forward.
Doesn't want to remember
the hanging insulation
in the baby's room
he was supposed to seal
before she came home from the hospital
or a month later
for no good reason
his clipboard from work
flying through the air
bruising the length of her leg.
She doesn't want to revisit
the midnight asthma runs
which ended the day she left the house
for a new life in another state
thinking the children would be healthier.
That is another story
she'd like to forget.

The Audio Engineer

He always had on him
wire cutters
a pair of pliers
plastic ties
a fountain pen and a pencil
a black clipboard
in the car an extension cord
headphones
cell phone for emergencies.
He was always dressed for the occasion.
If bicycling, bicycle shorts
a bicycle hat
water bottle
the right shoes.
He had all of it.
but seldom took the bike out.
Kept an album of pictures
of all his ex-girlfriends.
I'm probably in it now
in a separate ex-wife section.
He kept his CD's in alpha order
I'm talking ALL the letters.
I met a well-dressed man at a party once
had wire cutters on his belt.
"Are you an audio engineer?" I asked
"How did you know?"

OUT OF THE FRYING PAN

Divorce Rondelet

Break up, break down.
She tried to stay until the end.
Break up, break down.
She closeted the wedding gown.
There's only so far one can bend
only so much love to spend.
Break up, break down.

The Long "Y"

4-year-old's name
in pen on the porch rail
"Gaby"
the "y" etched the wood
all the way down
to the first floor
she was
grounded or spanked
(which?)
she swore
she didn't do it
to this day she swears
she didn't do it
I was afraid
to stand up
for my own
child
who was it
wrote her name
on the porch?

The Grandmother's Story

Her daughter married a second time
but the grandmother saw he was a bad man.

Knew the children were in danger.
She quit her job, moved closer.

Prayed morning and night.
Some nights she wasn't sure.

The daughter left once. When he
came to apologize, she went back.

The grandmother screamed
and tore her hair.

Three years went by until
her daughter left for good.

She held them in her arms,
her foolish daughter and her children.

The Pin

The four-year-old child running
arm hanging at her side.

The coach of the soccer team
turned out to be a doctor.

Helped put her in the car
arm across her belly.

The mother was wailing.
The husband told her to shut up.

The arrival at the hospital
The mother swallowing her fear.

The nurses taking the child to surgery
The husband leaving her there.

The doctor running out.
Giving her the keys to his car.

Sending her to another hospital
to pick up a smaller pin.

Her trip on the highway
in the doctor's BMW.

The look of shock on the nurse's face.
The delivery of the pin.

The child finally out of surgery
in traction, pin through her elbow.

The doctor thanking her.
We lost the brachial pulse for a moment there.

The mother imagining if she had come back
to hear her child was gone...

Sleeping in the child's hospital room.
Trying to keep a four-year-old calm for a week.

The pin coming out of the bone at 2am.
The mother assisting the doctor, nobody else was around.

The child screaming while she sang to her
holding her down.

The child brought back into surgery
emerging with a small, blue cast.

The husband coming to pick
them up with a sneer.

The mother, feeling empowered,
thinks about leaving him.

The child showing off
her hyper-extension.

Obituary for a Marriage

The husband would have said it died after the affair
for he made such a valiant effort
almost was able to forgive her
kept a close eye on her,
checked the mileage, the phone,
insisted she give up theater, music,
anything that might remind him
of her transgressions. After all, it was his right
to try to replace all the memories of her lover
with new ones of them both.
He made her take him to all the places
she had taken her lover for sex:
the woods by the bridge, the reservoir parking lot,
have sex with him there. She didn't complain.

The wife would have said it died after the wedding
he would spend hours on the computer
talking to strangers about religion,
while she cooked and cleaned, took care of five children,
his three from a first marriage, her two daughters.
When he was angry, he would hit her small daughter,
calling it a spanking, using all his strength.
The affair was a fantasy, a man who told her
she was talented, smart, beautiful.
She didn't even tell until she broke it off.
The guilt made her want to die.
He made her his slave for a year.
Then she said "enough, forgive me already."
Two more years before she found the courage
to rescue her child and what was left of her spirit.

the cat

a woman married a man
who pulled her close and closer
she fed him and his children

she cleaned their clothes their house
gave him her sex each night
he took all the love she had

she brought with her a white cat
a cat she used to love
the cat became very sick

the cat was skin and bones
he had her put it outside

all she could feel was fear
of his temper if she forgot
to feed the man or his children

the woman forgot to eat
forgot to feed the cat
the cat went into the woods
to die alone like cats do

the woman was skin and bones
was thinking she might die
then one day she woke up
remembering the cat

walked with her children
out of the woods
to live like women do

Awakening

I need you to

> bring me out of the rain
> shelter me with your words
> caress my trembling cheek
> repeat *it's all right, it's all right.*

The Corner of the Pantry

Crouching in the soft dark of the pantry
she slid down to sit along the cabinet wall.
Now she was safe and he was gone,
but once in a while a loud noise,
the shudder of the wind, or a memory
brought her back here again
to find the safe place in her mind.
Perhaps it was the smell of wood,
or the gentle rattle of dishes piled,
or because the cat would come
and rub against her arm, eye level,
as if he knew she needed him.

Inner Sky

That marriage was trees falling
ripped from their roots and flung,
felling her so hard she died
a little, so when she left
took time to clean him from her mind

where words resounded.
such as "stupid" and "can't"
You'd think the light, the slider doors
on her first apartment would have
made it easier, but nothing is easy.

She picked herself out of the piles
scattered along the path she'd cleared.
Without him she could see a flicker
of a girl who used to sing and write.
Some days the hands let go.
The part of her he corrupted
would come back and ruin things.

That freedom was inner sky
long warm days learning to live alone
made a decision to let go
to give herself permission
to ask herself, *what do I think?* to never
give her power to another again.

She knows her way now,
she sometimes even lends a hand
to others mired in storm.

The Ice Crow

carries my cage
on crooked back,
head bowed
focus forward,
black feet left tracks
across winter landscape.

Fishing pole tucked
under whitened wing;
tomorrow she plans to
lay down
her burdens
and mine

New Season

I am alive,
running over wet rocks
still tipped with
winter's frosting.
I almost slip,
barely holding on.
This is the key
to spring's return
along garden path,
already blooming
with forsythia, cherry.
Soon, marigolds
will ring tomatoes,
peppers, squash,
leaving winter
only a bookmark.

Acknowledgments

"Bitter Beets" appeared in Word Soup

About the Author

Lori Desrosiers' debut full-length book of poems, *The Philosopher's Daughter* was published by Salmon Poetry in 2013. *Sometimes I Hear the Clock Speak* will be out from Salmon in 2016. Her poems have appeared in *New Millenium Review, Contemporary American Voices, Best Indie Lit New England, String Poet, Blue Fifth Review, Pirene's Fountain, The New Verse News, The Mom Egg, The Bloomsbury Anthology of Contemporary Jewish-American Poetry* and many other journals and anthologies. Her work has been nominated for the 2015 Pushcart Prize. She won the Greater Brockton Poets Award for New England Poets award for her poem "That Pomegranate Shine" in 2010. She edits *Naugatuck River Review*, a journal of narrative poetry. She teaches Literature and Composition at Westfield State University and Holyoke Community College, and Poetry in the Interdisciplinary Studies program for the Lesley University M.F.A. graduate program.

GLASS LYRE PRESS, LLC
"exceptional works to replenish the spirit"

Poetry Collections
Poetry Chapbooks
Select Short & Flash Fiction
Anthologies

Glass Lyre Press is an independent literary publisher interested in technically accomplished, stylistically distinct, and original work. Glass Lyre seeks diverse writers that possess a dynamic aesthetic, and an ability to emotionally and intellectually engage a wide audience of readers.

Glass Lyre's vision is to connect the world through language and art. We hope to expand the scope of poetry and short fiction for the general reader through exceptionally well-written books, which evoke emotion, provide insight, and resonate with the human spirit.

www.GlassLyrePress.com

www.ingramcontent.com/pod-product-compliance
Lightning Source LLC
Chambersburg PA
CBHW060344080526
44584CB00013B/915